Chinese Designs and Motifs

Marty Noble

DOVER PUBLICATIONS, INC.
Mineola, New York

Copyright

Copyright © 2002 by Dover Publications, Inc.
All rights reserved under Pan American and International Copyright Conventions.

Bibliographical Note

Chinese Designs and Motifs is a new work, first published by Dover Publications, Inc., in 2002.

DOVER *Pictorial Archive* SERIES

This book belongs to the Dover Pictorial Archive Series. You may use the designs and illustrations for graphics and crafts applications, free and without special permission, provided that you include no more than four in the same publication or project. (For permission for additional use, please write to Permissions Department, Dover Publications, Inc., 31 East 2nd Street, Mineola, N.Y. 11501.)

However, republication or reproduction of any illustration by any other graphic service, whether it be in a book or in any other design resource, is strictly prohibited.

International Standard Book Number: 0-486-42307-7

Manufactured in the United States of America
Dover Publications, Inc., 31 East 2nd Street, Mineola, N.Y. 11501

Note

Over thousands of years–from fragments of sculpture found at neolithic sites, through the T'ang, Sung, Ming, Ch'ing and other great dynasties–Chinese art evolved into one of the world's major forms of artistic expression. Painting, calligraphy, ceramics, bronzes, jade and lacquerwork, silk, sculpture and other media have served Chinese artists as vehicles of expression for centuries. This collection of over 360 crisp, meticulously detailed motifs represents a rich cross-section of Chinese art and design, rendered by Marty Noble from authentic artifacts. Included are an enormous variety of patterns and designs, among them such traditional Chinese images as peacocks, cranes, dragons, demons, mythological figures, lanterns, fans, and many more. Also included is a wealth of florals, abstracts, repeat patterns, and ornament in a broad array of sizes and configurations: borders, ovals, rectangles, circles, rosettes and other shapes. Intricate, often highly stylized, Chinese designs lend themselves to a wide range of projects, including book and magazine illustration, wallpaper and textile design. The present collection, brimming with permission-free art, offers illustrators, graphic artists and craftworkers an extensive archive of designs for immediate practical use as well as an evergreen source of artistic inspiration.

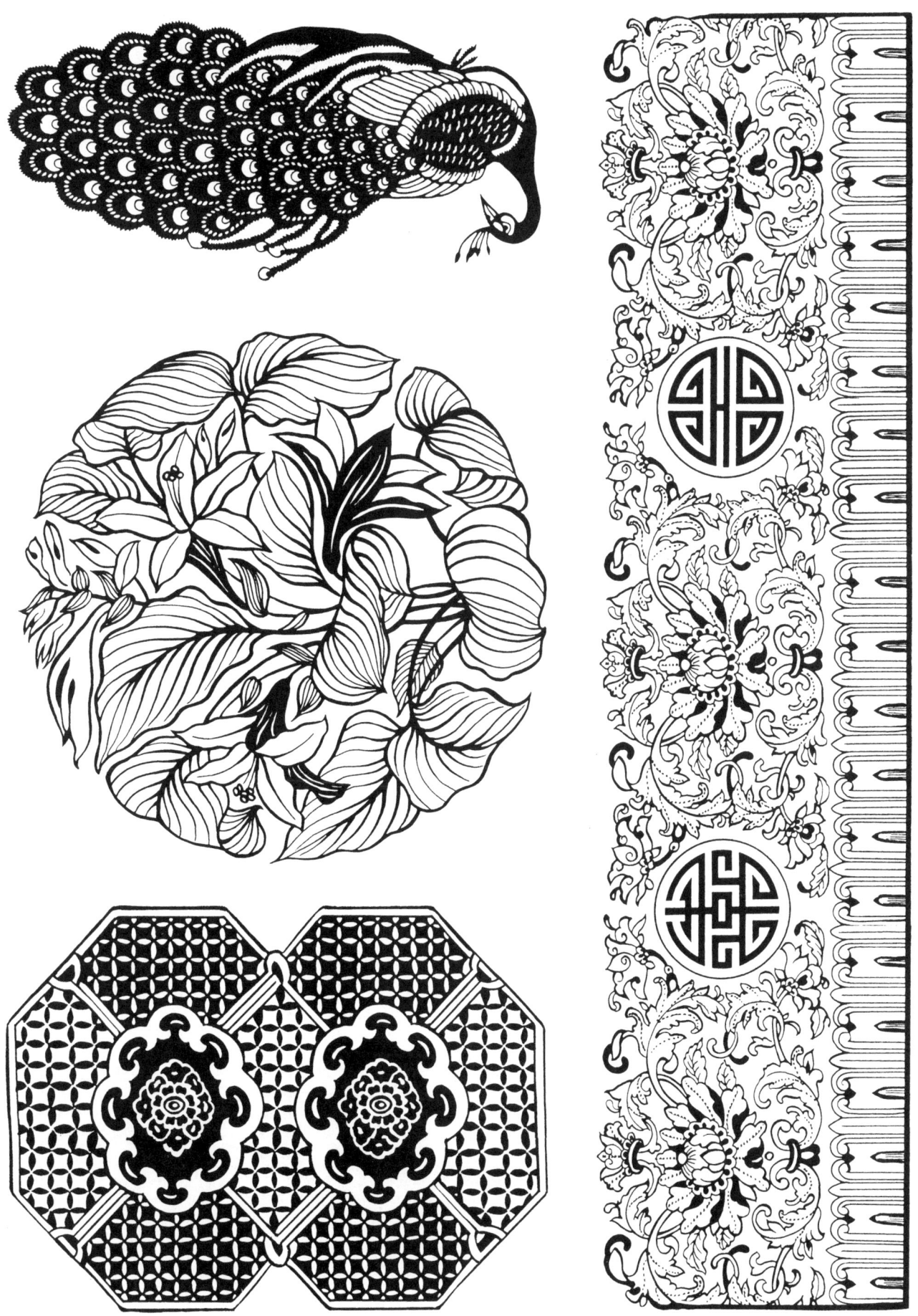

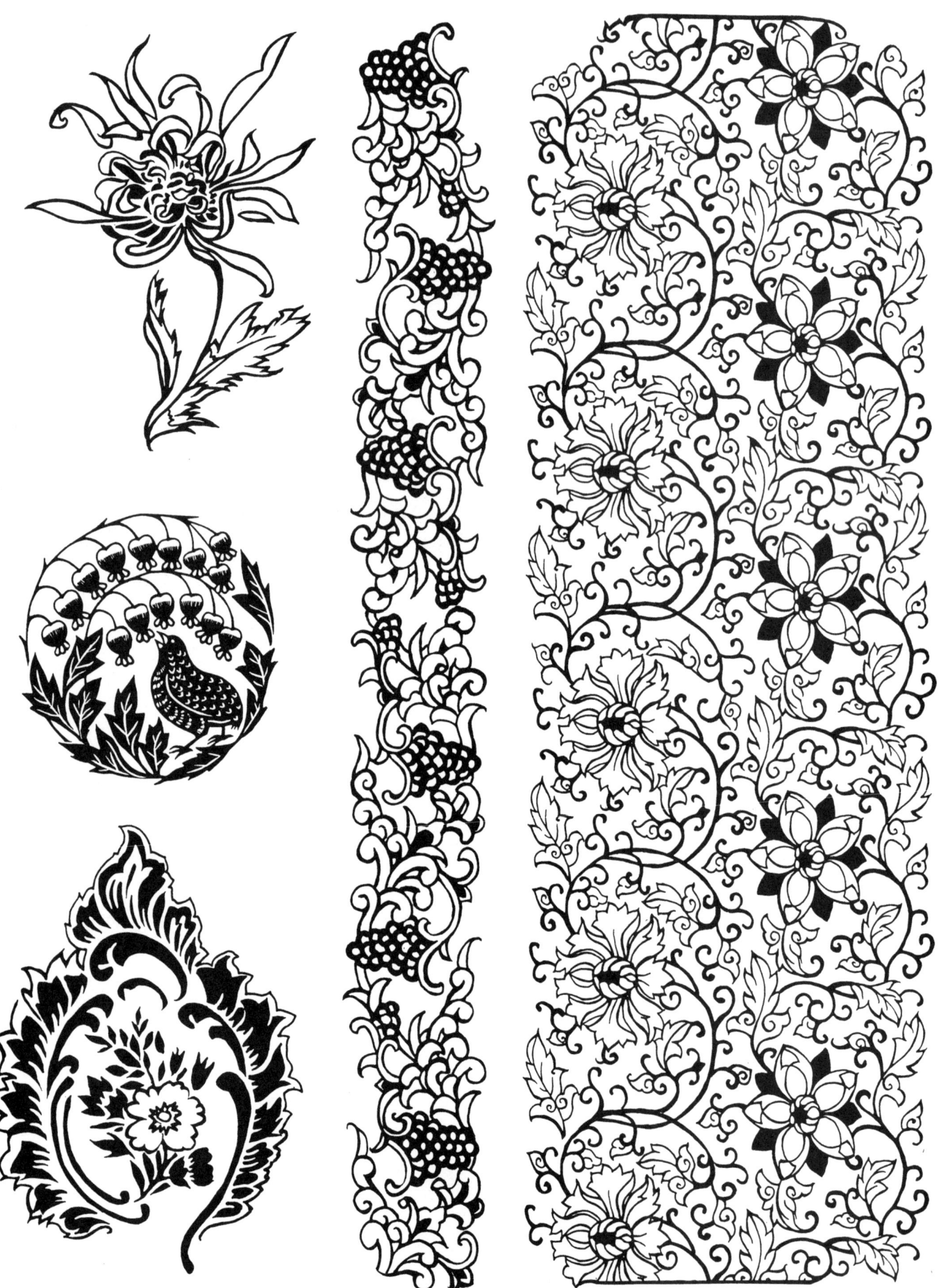

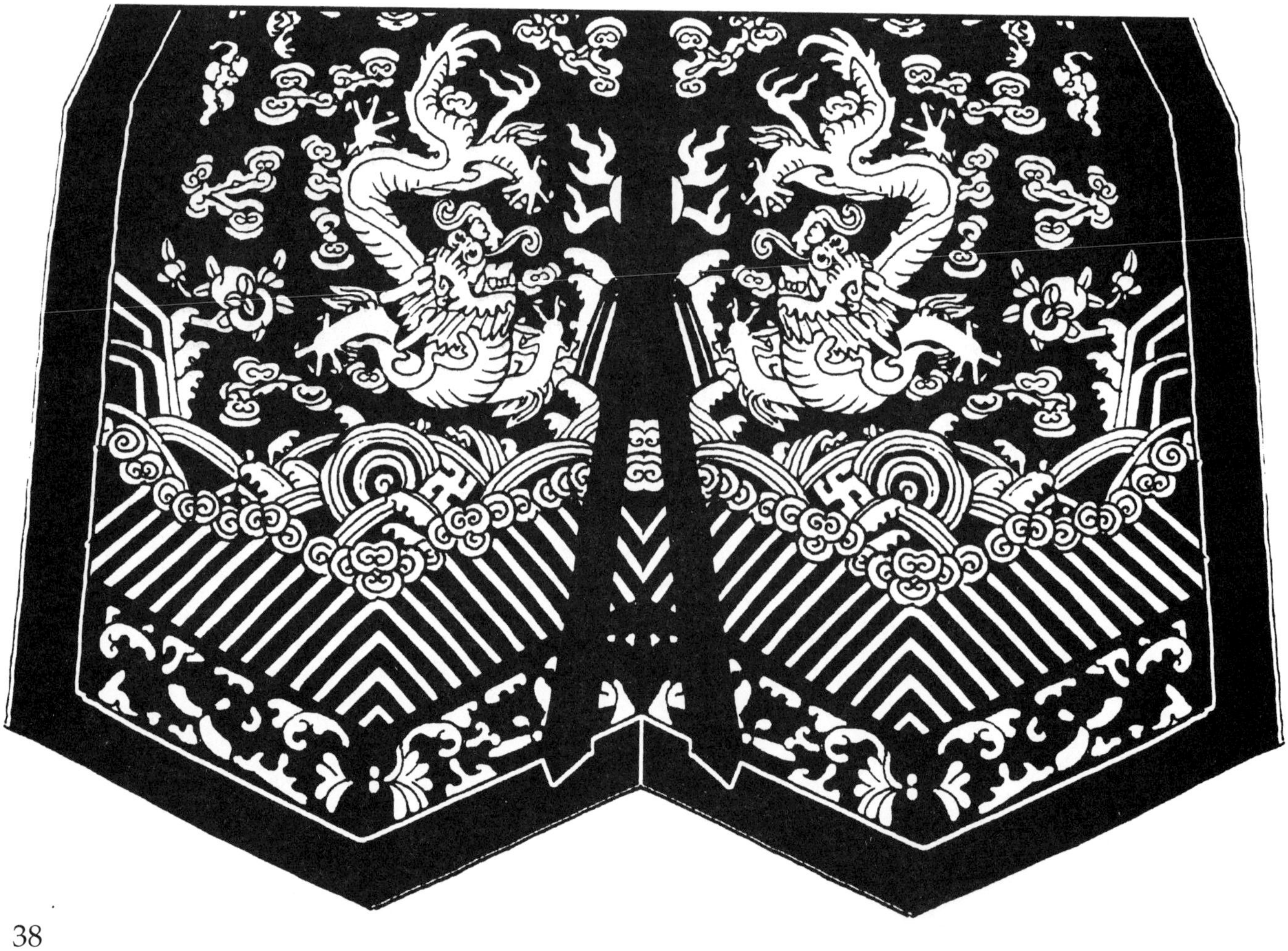

38

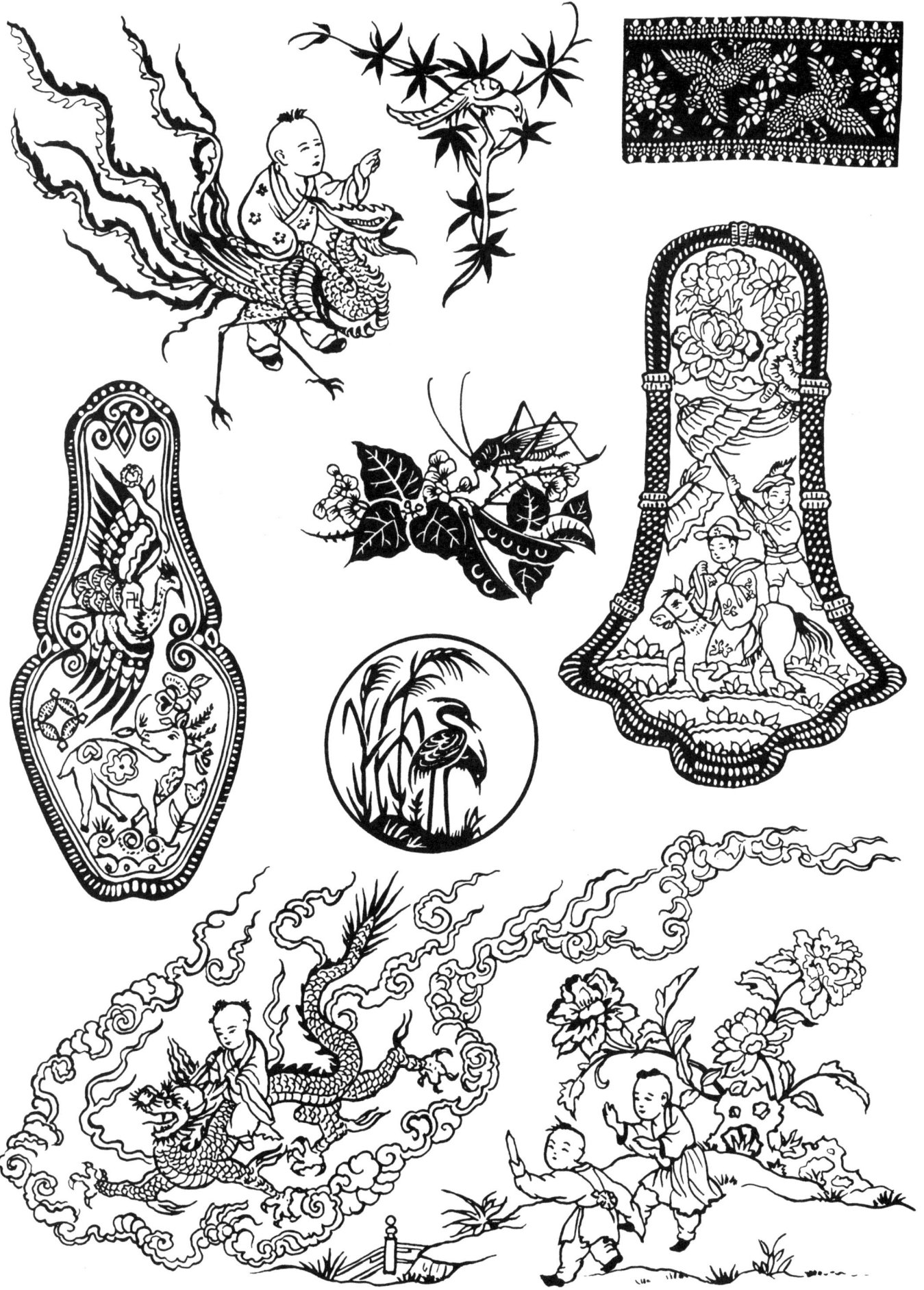

39

75